# Garbage Galore

## by Ellen Lawrence

**Consultants:**

**Darby Hoover**
Senior Resource Specialist
Natural Resources Defense Council, San Francisco, California

**Kimberly Brenneman, PhD**
National Institute for Early Education Research, Rutgers University
New Brunswick, New Jersey

BEARPORT
PUBLISHING

New York, New York

**Credits**

Cover, © Cathy Keifer/Shutterstock and Kanvag/Shutterstock; 2–3, © Inga Nielsen/Shutterstock; 4, © iStockphoto/Thinkstock and © BananaStock/Thinkstock; 5, © Dmitry Kalinovsky/Shutterstock; 6–7, © Rob Wilson/Shutterstock, © Risteski Goce/Shutterstock, © Sebastian Tomus/Shutterstock, and © Kanvag/Shutterstock; 8–9, © Kanvag/Shutterstock; 9, © Svetlana Kuznetsova/Shutterstock, © Lane V. Erickson/Shutterstock, © Nito/Shutterstock, © Matee Nuserm/Shutterstock, and © TigerForce/Shutterstock; 10, © auremar/Shutterstock; 11TL, © Aykut Erdogdu/Shutterstock; 11BL, © XXLPhoto/Shutterstock; 11R, © Africa Rising/Shutterstock; 12–13, © qingqing/Shutterstock; 13T, © herjua/Shutterstock; 14, © RTImages/Shutterstock, © Nito/Shutterstock, and © Somchai Som/Shutterstock; 15, © Jordache/Shutterstock; 15TR, © Jordache/Shutterstock; 15BR, © Levent Konuk/Shutterstock; 16T, © Cousin Avi/Shutterstock; 16B, © H. David Seawell/Corbis; 17, © Randy L. Rasmussen/The Oregonian; 18T, © Moreno Soppelsa/Shutterstock; 18B, © Africa Studio/Shutterstock; 19L, © Lourens Smak/Alamy; 19TR, © Franz-Peter Tschauner/Corbis; 20, © istockphoto/Thinkstock and © Monkey Business Images/Shutterstock; 21, © Valentin Agapov/Shutterstock, © Steve Lovegrove/Shutterstock, © Aleksandar Mijatovic/Shutterstock, © Stephen Mcsweeny/Shutterstock, © TigerForce/Shutterstock, © Ronald Sumners/Shutterstock, © photobank.ch/Shutterstock, © Dudarev Mikhail/Shutterstock, and © saiko3p/Shutterstock; 22T, © iStockphoto/Thinkstock; 22, © K. Miri Photography/Shutterstock, © hawkeye978/Shutterstock, © KariDesign/Shutterstock, and © tanewpix/Shutterstock; 23TL, © Sebastian Duda/Shutterstock; 23TR, © safakcakir/Shutterstock; 23B, © RTImages/Shutterstock.

**Publisher:** Kenn Goin
**Senior Editor:** Joyce Tavolacci
**Creative Director:** Spencer Brinker
**Design:** Emma Randall
**Editor:** Mark J. Sachner
**Photo Researcher:** Ruby Tuesday Books Ltd

*Library of Congress Cataloging-in-Publication Data*

Lawrence, Ellen, 1967– author.
  Garbage galore / by Ellen Lawrence.
      pages cm. — (Green world, clean world)
  Includes bibliographical references and index.
  ISBN 978-1-62724-102-1 (library binding) — ISBN 1-62724-102-7 (library binding)
 1. Refuse and refuse disposal—Juvenile literature. 2. Recycling (Waste, etc.)—Juvenile literature. 3. Pollution—Juvenile literature. I. Title.
  TD792.L39 2014
  363.72'82—dc23
                              2013041502

For more information, write to Bearport Publishing Company, Inc., 45 West 21st Street, Suite 3B, New York, New York 10010. Printed in the United States of America.

10 9 8 7 6 5 4 3 2 1

# Contents

Everyone Makes Garbage!......................4

Off to a Landfill...........................6

A Big Problem............................8

Recycling ...............................10

Saving Fossil Fuels and Energy................12

What Can a Can Become?...................14

Old Glass into New .......................16

Making Paper from Paper ...................18

Reduce, Reuse, Recycle .....................20


Science Lab ..............................22

Science Words ............................23

Index ..................................24

Read More ..............................24

Learn More Online ........................24

About the Author..........................24

# Everyone Makes Garbage!

Every day, people make garbage—and lots of it!

In one day, a family might throw away bottles, cans, and leftover food.

All of that trash is put into a garbage can and left on the curb.

Then a garbage truck takes the trash away, but where does it all go?

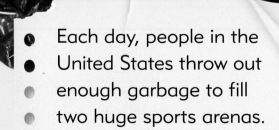

Each day, people in the United States throw out enough garbage to fill two huge sports arenas.

What do you think happens to your family's garbage once it's collected by a garbage truck?

# Off to a Landfill

garbage truck

After trucks collect garbage, they take it to a landfill.

A landfill is a large hole that is dug in the ground where garbage is buried.

Unfortunately, making a landfill uses up huge areas of land.

- When food scraps and yard waste, such as leaves, rot in landfills, they produce a gas called **methane**. Methane in the air is harmful. It traps the sun's heat and helps cause **global warming**.

❶ After a giant hole is dug in the ground, thick plastic sheets are laid inside it. This helps stop the garbage from spreading into other parts of the ground.

❷ Soil is put on top of the sheets. Then garbage is piled on top.

# Making a Landfill

methane collection plant

**4** At some landfills, methane is collected using special pipes. This stops it from escaping into the air.

**3** Workers cover the garbage with layers of soil.

7

# A Big Problem

Landfills cause a lot of **pollution**.

Some garbage, such as paint and glue, is made up of **chemicals**.

Chemicals in a landfill can leak into the ground.

They can pollute water under the soil that people, animals, and plants use.

When some chemicals in a landfill mix together, they can form poisonous gases.

The gases pollute the air and can make people who breathe them in sick.

Some garbage that is buried in a landfill quickly **decomposes**, or rots away. That's not true for all garbage, however. Many items take hundreds of years to break down!

◄ A banana peel may take only three to four weeks to decompose.

A newspaper ► may decompose in just six weeks.

◄ A metal can might take 100 years to break down.

Some scientists think ► that a plastic bottle could take more than 500 years to break into tiny pieces. However, the pieces might be in the ground forever.

◄ A glass jar may never decompose.

9

# Recycling

Landfills use up land, pollute, and leave garbage buried in the ground for a long time.

Some garbage doesn't have to go into landfills, though.

It can be **recycled**!

Recycling means turning used objects into something new.

For example, a used plastic bottle can be made into new plastic items.

Here's how!

**Recycling Plastic**

**1** Empty plastic bottles are put into a recycling bin.

**❷** Trucks take the bottles to a factory where they are washed to remove dirt and labels. A machine then grinds the bottles into tiny plastic flakes.

**❸** The flakes are melted and made into small beads called pellets.

**❹** Finally, the pellets are melted and the plastic is shaped into new items, such as new plastic bottles.

The plastic from a used bottle can be made into stuffing for pillows and sofas. It can also be used to make car bumpers and seats.

# Saving Fossil Fuels and Energy

It's better to recycle old plastic instead of making brand-new plastic. Why?

New plastic is made from **fossil fuels,** such as **natural gas** and oil, that are buried deep underground.

Collecting these fuels and transporting them to factories uses lots of **energy**.

Much of that energy is saved if new plastic is made from old plastic.

Turning old plastic into new plastic means that less natural gas and oil needs to be pumped from underground.

These machines are pumping oil that is underground.

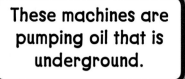
trucks delivering oil to a factory

Items that can be recycled often have this picture, or symbol, on them. What do you think the symbol is showing?
(The answer is on page 24.)

13

Like plastic bottles, cans can also be recycled.

Many cans are made from metals, such as steel and aluminum.

Items made from these metals can be recycled again and again.

A recycled can might be made into a new can.

It could also become paper clips— or even part of a skyscraper!

aluminum

Metal

steel

New steel is made by digging iron, limestone, and coal out of the ground. Then these materials are mixed together. Recycling old steel uses less new materials that have to be dug out of the ground.

# Recycling Steel Cans

**1** Used steel cans are taken to a steel plant. The cans are heated in a very hot oven where they melt and become liquid steel.

**2** As the liquid cools and becomes hard, it is shaped into large pieces of steel.

**3** The steel is rolled into sheets and is ready to be made into new steel items.

# Old Glass into New

Like plastic and metal, glass can be recycled over and over!

Most of the glass bottles and jars that are recycled become new bottles and jars.

It can take just 30 days to turn an old glass jar into a new one.

Here's how it's done.

## Recycling Glass

❶ Used glass items are taken to a factory where they are crushed.

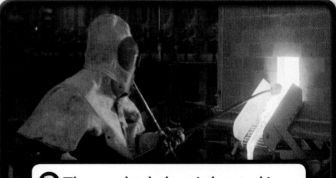

❷ The crushed glass is heated in a very hot oven where it melts and becomes liquid glass.

**3** The hot liquid glass is shaped into new items, such as jars and bottles.

These new glass bottles are still very hot.

New glass is made by melting and mixing sand, limestone, and a white powder called soda ash. Making new glass from old glass doesn't use up more of these materials.

17

# Making Paper from Paper

Paper is another material that can be recycled.

When a newspaper is recycled, it might be made into a new newspaper in just seven days!

Old paper can be turned into the pages of a book or even toilet paper.

Here's what happens to recycled paper at a **paper mill**.

used paper at a paper mill

How many paper items does your family throw away? For one week, collect any clean, used paper that your family throws out. Count how many pieces of paper you have collected. Make sure you recycle all the paper at the end of the week!

18

# Recycling Paper

**1** At a paper mill, used paper is washed to remove any ink. The wet, mushy paper is called pulp.

**2** A machine squashes the pulp into flat sheets.

**3** The water is squeezed from the sheets, and then they are dried. Now the old paper has become new paper.

Paper is made from trees. When recycled paper is made from used paper, fewer trees need to be cut down.

# Reduce, Reuse, Recycle

Recycling is one way to keep garbage from going into landfills.

People can also try to reduce the amount of garbage they make.

Reusing items instead of throwing them away also makes less trash.

Reducing, reusing, and recycling are known as the three Rs.

If everyone follows the three Rs, our world will be a greener, cleaner place!

Every year, the amount of plastic bags and plastic wrap used in the United States weighs more than ten Empire State Buildings! Instead of wrapping food, put it into a reusable plastic box.

# Reduce

When you are in a grocery store, look at how much packaging an item has. A lot of packaging ends up in landfills, so buy items with less packaging.

**lots of packaging**

**no packaging**

Draw or write on both sides of a piece of paper.

# Reuse

Carry groceries in reusable cloth bags instead of paper or plastic bags that get thrown away.

Look at this empty glass jar. Write a list of ways that you could reuse the jar. How many can you think of?

# Recycle

Cut up old clothes into rags. Use the rags to dry dishes or clean up messes.

Use clean, empty yogurt cups as flowerpots. Make three holes in the bottom of a cup to allow water to drain out. Fill the cup with potting soil, then plant your seeds.

**21**

# Science Lab

A lot of the garbage that goes into landfills is leftover food and yard waste. However, this type of garbage can be turned into compost, a special kind of soil that keeps plants healthy and helps them grow faster. You can make your own compost in a few steps.

**You will need:**

- An adult helper
- A pair of scissors
- An old plastic box with a lid
- Leftover food and yard waste for composting
- Potting soil
- A small shovel

**Use only the following to make compost:**

- Vegetables and fruits
- Bread, pasta, and rice
- Coffee grounds
- Tea bags
- Egg shells
- Grass and plant clippings
- Fall leaves
- Brown paper bags
- Used paper towels

**NEVER put meat or fish in your compost bin.**

## How to Make a Compost Bin and Compost

**❶** Ask an adult to use scissors to make a few small holes in the bottom of a plastic box to allow water to drain out.

**❷** Then have the adult make about ten dime-sized holes in each side of the box to let air in. Stand the box on a patch of ground.

compost bin

**❸** Place some compost materials in the box. Put some potting soil on top. Close the box's lid.

**Always wash your hands with soap and warm water after working with compost.**

compost materials

**❹** Every day, add more compost materials.

**❺** About once a month, use a small shovel to stir up and turn the compost.

**❻** Be patient. It will take several months for your garbage to turn into rich compost. Then you can sprinkle it around plants to help them grow!

compost

# Science Words

**chemicals**
(KEM-uh-kuhlz)
substances made by
people that can be
harmful to living things

**decomposes**
(*dee*-kuhm-POHZ-iz)
rots or breaks down into another form

**energy** (EN-ur-jee)  power, such as electricity,
that machines and vehicles need in order
to work

**fossil fuels** (FOSS-uhl FYOO-uhlz)  fuels, such
as coal, oil, and natural gas, that formed deep
underground from the remains of plants and
animals that died millions of years ago

**global warming** (GLOHB-uhl WARM-ing)
the slow and steady heating up of Earth's air
and oceans caused by certain gases that trap
the sun's heat in Earth's atmosphere

**methane** (METH-ayn)  a type of gas that has no
smell or color and is made when garbage, such
as food, decomposes; one of the gases that
causes global warming

**natural gas** (NACH-ur-uhl GASS)  a type of
fossil fuel that is buried deep underground
and can be used to power stoves

**paper mill** (PAY-pur MIL)
a factory where paper is made

**pollution** (puh-LOO-shuhn)
materials, such as trash
and chemicals, that can
damage the air, water,
and soil

**recycled** (ree-SYE-kuhld)
when old, unwanted objects
are turned into something
new

# Index

aluminum 14
cans 4, 9, 14–15
chemicals 8
composting 22
energy 12
fossil fuels 12
garbage trucks 4–5, 6

glass 9, 16–17, 21
global warming 6
landfills 6–7, 8–9, 10, 20
methane 6–7
natural gas 12
oil 12–13
paper 9, 18–19, 21, 22

plastic 6, 9, 10–11, 12, 14, 16, 20–21, 22
pollution 8, 10
recycling 10–11, 12–13, 14–15, 16–17, 18–19, 20–21, 22
steel 14–15
three Rs 20–21

# Read More

**Lepetit, Angie.** *Trash Magic: A Book about Recycling a Plastic Bottle (Earth Matters).* North Mankato, MN: Capstone (2013).

**Metz, Lorijo.** *What Can We Do About Trash and Recycling? (Protecting Our Planet).* New York: Rosen (2010).

# Learn More Online

To learn more about garbage, visit
www.bearportpublishing.com/GreenWorldCleanWorld

# About the Author

Ellen Lawrence lives in the United Kingdom. Her favorite books to write are those about nature and animals. In fact, the first book Ellen bought for herself, when she was six years old, was the story of a gorilla named Patty Cake that was born in New York's Central Park Zoo.

# Answer for Page 13

The three sections of the symbol stand for the three stages of recycling.

1) An item is collected for recycling.
2) It goes to a recycling plant.
3) The item is made into something new.

The symbol shows the three stages happening again and again in a cycle, or circle.